Jeannine Hall Gailey's *Field Guide to the End of the World* crackles with wit, wonder, and wisdom. Her primer for the end days shows us how the world is always ending--there are plenty of disasters to go around. But these poems aren't a slog through the wasteland. They're funny, thoughtful meditations on how each of us survives the world's end--every single day of our lives.

—Ryan Teitman, author *Litany for the City*

"The end of the world has never been so full of life. *Field Guide to the End of the World* continues to showcase Gailey's masterful and inimitable talent for marrying the sublime world of imagination with the gritty flesh of reality. This collection is the latest opus of a poet at the height of her powers."

—Jason Mott, author of *The Returned*

Jeannine Hall Gailey's *Field Guide to the End of the World* is a smart, dark confrontation of catastrophe—what it means for a culture, and what it means for the individual. Martha Stewart gathers drones and lemons, and reminds us, "Survival skills are just like hostess skills." But can one person's regressive malfunction can be another's progressive mutation? Invoking fairy tales and science fictions in equal measure, the author prods at what it means when "Your body is the tower you long to escape" and, on a later page, "Like a radio   some of my connections have gone bad   fizzled." These poems are mesmerizing in their music, their humor, and their eye for the exact right details to inspire hope while acknowledging ruin. The last love poem still conspires to bake cookies, to plant dahlias. "If I smell the air I can believe," declares the joyfully defiant "Post-Apocalyptic Postcard from Appalachian Chalet." I've gravitated to peri-apocalyptic narratives for as long as I could read, and followed Gailey's work for over a decade, and I can say without hesitation: this is the best of both.

—Sandra Beasley, author of *Count the Waves and I Was the Jukebox*

Field Guide to the End of the World

by Jeannine Hall Gailey

MOON CITY PRESS
Department of English
Missouri State University
901 South National Avenue
Springfield, Missouri 65897

First Edition
Copyright © 2016 by Jeannine Hall Gailey
All rights reserved.
Published by Moon City Press, Springfield, Missouri, USA, in 2015.

Library of Congress Cataloging-in- Publication Data

Gailey, Jeannine Hall, 1973-

Field guide to the end of the world: poems/Jeannine Hall Gailey

Library of Congress Control Number: 2016909947

Further Library of Congress information is available upon request.

ISBN-10 0913785768
ISBN-13: 978-0913785768

Text edited by Sara Burge
Text copyedited by Karen Craigo
Cover designed by Charli Barnes
Interior designed by Kyle Rutherford

Manufactured in the United States of America.

www.mooncitypress.com

Acknowledgments for
Field Guide to the End of the World

I would like to thank my wonderful editors at Moon City Press, Sara J. Burge and Michael G. Czyzniejewski.

I would like to thank Charli Barnes for her work on the cover art and design of this book.

Many thanks to the Helen R. Whiteley Center at Friday Harbor Laboratories residency program for their support while writing this book.

Thanks to the Jack Straw Writing Residency Program for their support during the writing of this book.

Thanks to my husband Glenn Allen Gailey and to my family: my parents, Drs. Bettie and Ernest Hall, and my three brothers, Michael Duke Hall, Charles Brett Hall, and Donald Scott Hall.

Thanks to my poet friends who provided so much support during the writing of this book: Kelli Russell Agodon, Kelly Davio, Annette Spaulding-Convy, Jenifer Lawrence, Natasha K. Moni, Holly Hughes, Ronda Broatch, and Lana H. Ayers.

I'd like to gratefully acknowledge all the journals where these poems first appeared.

- "Sentient or Replicant," appeared in *Hayden's Ferry Review*.
- "Post-Apocalypse Postcard (with HGTV Magazine) appeared on *The Rumpus*, April 2015.
- "Field Guide to the End of the World," "In Case," and "Post-Apocalypse Postcard with Anthropologie Catalogue" appeared in *Front Porch*.
- "But It Was an Accident" appeared in *The Cincinnati Review*.
- "Notes Before the Apocalypse" and "Introduction to Salvation" appeared in *Moon City Review*.
- "Introduction to the Parables of Jesus" appeared in *The Cossack Review*.
- "Post-Apocalypse Postcard with American Girl" and "Remnant" appeared in *Tinderbox*.
- "Introduction to Electromagnetics" and "To the Ends of the Earth" appeared in *Mythic Delirium*.
- "Introduction to Field Studies" appeared in *Redactions*.
- "Every Human is a Black Box" appeared in *Mid-American Review*.

- "Introduction to Ruby Slippers, Hot Air Balloons" appeared in *FreezeRay*.
- "Introduction to Dream Interpretation" appeared in *Redactions*.
- "The Last Love Poem" appeared in *Linebreak*.
- "Introduction to the Limits of Metaphor (a Love Poem)" appeared on *The Rumpus*, April 2014.
- "Introduction to Junk Science" appeared in *The Tahoma Review*.
- "Epilogue" appeared in *Redactions*.
- "For the Love of Ivy" appeared in *Barrelhouse's* online superhero issue.
- "Introduction to Disaster" appeared in *Poet's Market 2014*.
- "Introduction to Alien Autopsy" appeared in *Eye to the Telescope*.
- "Introduction to Time Travel Theory" appeared in *Apex and Abyss*.
- "Introduction to Sex and Death" appeared in vol 2. of *Archaeopteryx*.
- "Introduction to Teen Girl Vampires" appeared in *Hobble Creek Review*.
- "Introduction to the Body in Fairy Tales" appeared in *Phantom Drift*, and was included in *The Best Horror of the Year Vol 6*.
- "Hedy Lamarr Told to Stop Silly Inventing" appeared in *Escape into Life*.
- "Introduction to California Poetics" appeared on *LA Weekly*, online feature, May 5, 2011.
- "If I Stayed in Kansas, I Knew My Future" appeared in *Anti-*.
- "Introduction to Algebra" and "Introduction to Witchcraft" appeared in *Atticus Review*.
- "Introduction to Mutagenesis" appeared in *The Pedestal*.
- "Introduction to Engineering from Wile E. Coyote, Supergenius" appeared in *Stone Highway Review*.
- "Introduction to Your Own Personal Genome Project" appeared in January 2015's issue of *Mythic Delirium*. "Zombie Stripper Clones: They Are Not Regenerating" won the Lizzy Acker Monster Poetry Contest in 2010 and was featured on the *We Who Are About to Die* web site. *Post-Apocalypse Postcard from the Viceroy Hotel* appeared in *The Pedestal Magazine*.

TABLE OF CONTENTS

Disaster Studies

Introduction to Disaster Preparedness

While you told me about the bee colony collapse
caused by cell phones or maybe Monsanto and their magic poisons

I was thinking about a friend who said *they found a lump*
and another friend finishing chemo and waiting for a scan

and a third who said *my hair is a disaster* and she meant the layers
would take forever to grow out. *My house is a disaster,* she says, *my yard, my outfit.*

When you told me *my son is autistic* I thought of his bright eyes
and beautiful tears. It's not the life you planned. How our minds

and bodies spin apart, like hives of bees confused about whom to follow,
flying further and further out to discover – what? That they'd flown

too far and now are frozen, flightless. How many hives abandoned.
We cannot sleep too far from disaster zones. I saw a tornado once

in my own front yard, and slept through hurricanes, knelt during earthquakes.
Did I pray, did I ask for something then? I only held my breath.

When later asked, *Are you okay?* I said, *Everything is temporary.*

Field Guide to the End of the World

If you study the crop circles and the mutations of frogs
long enough, they will whisper their secrets

in the code of alien DNA. If you build a bunker underground,
weigh carefully those you invite to share it. Rent an RV

and a ham radio. Visions of being lifted up to Heaven?
Maybe a trip with the family to the seaside?

Break into an underground military mountainside
with just two orphans and a shotgun,

swearing you have the salt that will heal the sick.
You've always been a thinker. Keep your notebook and pencil:

someone will have to record a history of plagues and patient zeros.
Listen to the songs of children around the fire, their wee voices

calling giant caterpillars, nuclear forests and flying squirrels.
The Kingdom may already be at hand. Marshal your resources.

Keep a steady eye on the whirling dervish of the sun,
straining its rays towards us to blind or protect.

Are We There Yet?

In these close cramped quarters we travel
together, the human race, one man kicking the seat
and another, too close, pinching my arm.

The sky-blue Plymouth of our lives is lined
in sticky vinyl and no one is playing the music
I like. Overhead the screams of vultures, but someone

shouts *It's a hawk!* And someone else is playing
twenty questions, asking *What is the mind of God?*
Which way are we heading?

Careening down a freeway with few signs
or wonders, we do our best to stay focused
on enjoying the journey, distracting ourselves

with games, whistling in the dark. You and I
pass the crayons back and forth, telling each other
once more the story of creation, stories of genomes,

while the kind rabbits scramble over hills out of the sun.
Squabbling, we're in a hurry to reach the end of our journey,
settle down in our final destination.

Post-Apocalypse Postcard from the Viceroy Hotel, Santa Monica

I woke up and laid out by the pool, still blue and inviting, the swim-up bar emptied of everything but ice buckets. Oh, for ice. There was something falling from the sky, tiny and white, but it wasn't snow. It was ashes. Ashes of what? The roses were blooming outside the gate, just like always. The sky, a true LA muted gray, just as oppressive as that August we visited. Remember the flashfires, everything up in smoke, the canyons a trap, no one left to run to the ocean? I've been living on nuts and pretzels, upscale liquor stuck in locked minibars, orange juice for breakfast, chocolate and vodka at night. I haunt the hotel in robes and slippers, wrap myself in sheets, with no one left to watch. I walked to Fred Segal, the poor sad mannequins, the lipsticks scattered on the floor, the size two tank tops hanging empty on the racks. There were still flavored syrups at the Coffee Bean; almond, raspberry. The flowers haven't crumpled to nothingness yet, though the lawns are brown and the fountains stopped their splashing. Ashes, ashes, they all fall down.

Introduction to Mutagenesis

This is the secret: mostly our mutations are hidden under skin.
On the outside, robust and rosy as a milkmaid; inside, not entirely stable.

Errors in replication – beyond our control – and yet sometimes the systemic destruction
of a certain cell might lead to a breakthrough, a land mass not yet discovered inside us,

clever adaptations that let us survive genetic drift in cases of plague or flood,
carriers of one disease not susceptible to another, heme content falling or rising

according to the prevalent virus. Yes, the one-eyed kitten, that six-legged Chernobyl calf,
but more often…me, girl with heritable deficiencies and tendencies.

There is misconception about mutants, but we don't sprout doll's heads from our wrists,
octopus tentacles, though perhaps, yes, the occasional vestigial tail.

But don't feel sorry for us. We don't live some half-life, waiting for our inner monster
to be revealed. Maybe we revel in our inner demon, the dragon inside

and anyway, how can you be so sure you're so pure, so uncontaminated?
Inside us each ticks the act of betrayal, the strand of DNA unraveling –

you're one incident away from being my perfect match, my beautiful mutant.

Martha Stewart's Guide to Apocalypse Living

Of course you know I love those little drones, so I've stockpiled them. Those and lemons. I've learned the hard way that life without lemons is barely worth living.

Animal husbandry 101: Fill your own organic pantry. Which breed of chicken will give you the best eggs under stress? Pg. 13.

Leave the fondant til later. You can always do a ganache topping for your cupcakes in a pinch. So simple!

Evacuation map for New York City, Boston, the Hamptons, with scratch-and-sniff icons: page 24.

Survival skills are just like hostess skills: a little preparation, a little spying with the drones, a little determined defense-driven hedging of the grounds. Razor wire goes beautifully with your holly thicket.

Guide to storing munitions in attractive wicker boxes: page 52.

If your water isn't as clear as it should be, use up those charcoal filters first, but after, try a solid iodine tablet in your home-dug well. In these times, it's a good thing.

Culinary tips for after the mega-store raid: Mixed nuts have a long shelf life. Throw in a little rosemary and toast them over an open flame for anytime elegance. More ideas for those family-sized tubs of popcorn: page 68.

Now's the time to get out your hurricane lamps! They create a lovely glow in these last days.

In Case

We were taught in grade school different lessons of survival:
In case of nuclear attack, hide under your desk.
In case of chemical attack, buy duct tape.
Buy a rape whistle. Carry knives. Learn a martial art.

I read old fairy tales, wolves lurking behind trees
and parents ready to kill children. Magic mirrors,
dragons, spells that charm and protect.
Burn this herb to banish ghosts.

Sometimes I imagine the afterlife, puffs of pink
clouds and unicorns, or gold harps, or glass cities
with streets made of emerald. The whole earth
spinning like a child's marble below, pitiful.

We are told to vaccinate, to educate, to warn.
Traffic tickets, parking signs: bureaucratic safety nets.
Our governments promise safety in exchange for...
I will light a candle, listen to the solar-charged radio for a sign.

Burning In, Burning Out:
A 4th of July Meditation on Neural Lesions

The sparklers fizzle and burn in the front yard, the screams of children
as stray embers land on their arms and legs, spinning in the hot air

like my rebellious neurons sputter their signal from one end to the next,
refusing to move muscle fibers in one direction.

An imagined apocalypse inside the body, the stink of sulfur and saltpeter in the air;
the splashes of light around you, real or imagined?

The twitching is the failed ignition. Turn the key but all you hear is a grinding
     sound
coming from the motor. Your system is less reliable, a fancy Italian sports car

on the fritz: sleek and red and shiny, but ultimately broken down. Your mind is a
     flame
about to go out. Burning inward, not out, burning along the lines of your body,

starting at the fingers, reaching your spine, your lips, your tongue.
The feeling of sparklers fizzling along your skin, your embers dying.

Every Human is a Black Box

We all carry our own map to disaster, the faint voice recordings
that veer from mundane to hysterical in that last moment.
There's no turnkey solution to us; one person's milk
is another's poison; my mother swears green tea gives her hives.

My husband looks up from the field with scratchy throat and red eyes,
while I frolic in amid the goldenrod; at night I toss and wheeze
in the dust of my pillow while he snores dreamlessly.

Our lives have stood, like loaded guns – for one, heart attack
by sauce alfredo, for another, 101 years of béarnaise and tobacco
troubled by nothing more than mild glaucoma. Some of us
can disregard the warnings; others must cling tightly to directions.

When you slide into the grave, remember your body is a document,
a reminder, a memorial to distant waters, the siren call of cells
to sleep. Turn off. Shut down. Mayday, May Day.

Introduction to the Limits of Metaphor
(A Love Poem)

I am snowing inside I am a house with a rickety dodgy roof
I am a boat that is capsizing I am the waves cold on your feet

You are the moon you are what I reach for
I am the cranberry in your tart you are the splinter from the wood spoon

You have a face like a coin
I am the fingertip on the window

You are rain you are a storm surge you have devastated
you are the peel of the apple I am the blackberry juice on your lips

you are the peacock's screech I am somnolent as night doves
you are traffic jams I am a desert road

I have a wool sweater on my heart
you wear socks on your voice box

I am red lipstick you are the pair of shoes that goes with nothing in the closet
you are an untidy and scorched omelet I am a fallen soufflé

I am season one of Lost you are season nine of the X Files
I am missing organs I am the fallen starlet you are the boy born without a face

we are a pile of fur and feathers leather and oil stain
Civet cat and cigarette perfume wine glass and poorly knit rug

I am cesium I am a radon daughter
you are the phosphorous glow you are the sodium flame

we are teenagers in the rain speeding cars tumbles in the corn
we are empty bottles in morning light with labels torn off we are wingless fireflies
we are outlying data the graph that goes off the charts

I am snowing I am out of your reach I am a seascape on your wall
I am a boat gone missing on your horizon

Post-Apocalypse Postcard
(with Anthropologie Catalog)

I've always wanted to be one of those girls in an Anthropologie catalog, the kind with their lank hair crowned casually with $300 faux-metal tiaras and tipping up their $1,000 hand-crafted tree toppers.

And now here, this desert landscape lends itself to exactly that – emaciated and pale under tents, we stand and wait for the sun with expressions hinting of some future pleasure. Our hammock is festooned with festive scarves, and seashells serve ice from our last buckets. One more willow branch to mark the day; these strappy leather sandals perfect for sand-charred paths, and someone is lounging against an antique cello casually, as if about to play music.

We don't worry about the ruined maps, the coffee cups staining the fabrics we've acquired so painstakingly, now. We don't plan for anything.

We're looking picturesque, holding a woven bamboo suitcase as the future dissipates like a $40 fig fragrance diffuser, the children concentrating on braiding bracelets, all of our jaunty sunglasses stacked against the glare of the coming—

Lessons in Emergency

Learn to break glass to take what you need with you when you go

Learn to tie shoes quickly to find the emergency medications the rations the earthquake kit

Is it in your car that you feel safest? Your house? Are you one more Lois Lane with sand coming in the windows trying to break the glass? Are you waiting for some Superman are you waiting?

In the strictest sense, what can you live without? Water food toilet paper a toothbrush your laptop your cat your husband your little boy your wait a second what am I forgetting?

Quick! The sirens are blaring you shove your palms over your ears - where do you take cover?

Do you ever watch your landscape and wonder where it might collapse? Buildings, tunnels, forest groves, bridges. When you watch the earth tear apart like thin skin you think briefly *everything is so fragile.*

In the end you are still yourself, yourself a little dustier a little blood in the hair maybe a bit rattled but why are you clutching the egg-beater in your hands so tight, your fingers still touched with flour? You ask yourself: is now the time for cake?

Frank O'Hara tells you to become a blonde, as religious as a profligate Frenchman. You slip his words in your pocket and run.

Post-Apocalypse Postcard from an American Girl

Back in her childhood bedroom, she can't decide what to pack – the Tom Petty and Elvis records, her ticket stubs from American Idol? Ancient icons – the flag, her baton, her majorette costume – seem less useful now than Tupperware, aspirin, Bactine and Band-Aids. She longed for her mother to tell her once again what to do – not to wear her bangs too long, or her skirt too short. Not to wear too much lipstick. She was thankful for her lessons from summer camp – cooking eggs in a skillet over a fire, learning to shoot a shotgun at seven, and her aim was still true despite skinny arms. She could still sing the Star Spangled Banner with the best of them. Beneath the wild eyes of her faded toy horses, the blank grey faces of dead television sets, she dreams once more of a little more life, somewhere else. She ties the laces of her rollerblades tight, determined for once to do much more than survive.

Cultural Anthropology

Post-Apocalypse Postcard with Food Network Hostess

Dear Ina, thanks for having us out to the Hamptons, the perfect getaway – so few screams out on the coast, away from prying eyes. Loved the set of guest soaps, precious these days, the sprigs of lavender and thyme, the basket of strawberry muffins with preserved lemon butter. Jeffrey's sweater comes in handy these cold nights, and his tips on the global economy right on target, plus, your anecdotes about nuclear policy in the 80s - hilarious. You taught me how to harvest sea salt from the ocean, how to coax flavor from smoked salmon. And if anyone can make cooking over a fire seem cozy, it's you! The orange yolks of your organic eggs made me think of the old days, my mother's harried breakfasts, the bit of silver in her hair. Your starched blue eyes crinkle just like hers, your bob still spotless even without electricity. The lights over the harbor seem so benign out here. The chilled sunshine leaving its dying rays on your face as we waved goodbye, good luck, barefoot on the wrecked beach.

Introduction to Engineering
by Wile E. Coyote, Super Genius

In some mythologies, the coyote is the cleverest of species, constant in his menace
and cunning. The coyote can trick even the gods, hold the moon in his teeth.

But here, sadly, we see the lame duck physicist, the robotic designer
whose creations never quite reach the desired conclusions;

programming punch cards, the coyote reads his own doom –
once again to be crushed under the weight of his own machine.

We learn here to be skeptics, technology versus speed, cross-dressing
and baited traps. We imagine, as he balances his vial of TNT,

the years of failed research grants behind him, the lectures given at night
to overweight men with beards and smeared glasses, their reflections empty

as his own expectations. Why does the coyote want to eat the roadrunner,
that skinny and unluscious phantom, that puff of smoke? Why hold up tiny signs

asking vainly for help? When he sues Acme, how can we not applaud?
After so many drops off canyon cliffs, autos and rockets dragging him over cacti

and red rock, can't we wish him well, his continual look of surprise a reminder of
even
the most sophisticated scientist's helplessness in the throes of desire, unsatiated
appetite?

Letter to John Cusack, Piloting a Plane in an Apocalypse Movie

Dear John,

Let me say first of all how proud I am that we have both made it so far. I thought for sure I was a goner in that earthquake, plus radioactive lizards, and the way you flew through the crumbling tunnels and crashing skyscraper? Amazing! I'd like to ask you about the old map the crazy mountaineer gave you, the arks they built in China, and really, are you still kickboxing? Because it really did become sport of the future. You were right. I never believed you loved dogs, though. You seem more like a cat guy, furtive and light on your feet. Your mistrust of drones a prescient peek into the robot rebellion. Since we're at the end of civilization, I suppose we must finally shed our black trench coats and bad attitudes, because why be subversive, anymore? We must create our own shiny new future, maybe featuring spaceships. We must hold the cornerstones of civilization above us, like a boombox, and maybe Peter Gabriel can teach us once again how to be human, offer one another the comfort of a corner of the sad blanket we must finally share, shivering, in the rain at the dusk of mankind's existence.

Love,
The Girl from the Barn You Saved from Alien Hunters

Introduction to Spy Narrative as Love Story

When I look in a mirror all I see is you
written across my body like the shadow of a blackbird
which is, of course, your code name. I've hidden my gun

in a container of ice cream that's calling me
insistently as we waltz through a crowd and I tug a key
from inside your jacket and pull away for the dead drop.

And when all I got was two shots to the heart -
well, I knew what kind of dance this was from the beginning,
because what kind of person puts themselves in harm's way

every day, some kind of hero? Who do you think you are?
Sure, you can jump out of a plane or pass the polygraph
while singing my favorite song, the one you sing in the shower

when you think no one hears, but I've been tracking your moves
and kept the paperwork hidden. All that's needed now is for someone
to take your badge and call for the burn notice.

Your kiss was always so cold. I didn't even notice the hollow
ache you left. Let's dance. You shot me down, bang bang.
One more body from a moving train. It's time

at last to switch allegiances, identities, change costumes and passports
before I become one more silhouette forgotten, one more asset turned
agent provocateur, blowback from missing your hard target.

Introduction to Teen Witchcraft

Always these young women in search of power,
their eyes rolled back in their heads, midriffs exposed.

Always some girl with a candle in a dark room –
and poof, her face brightens as she achieves some moment

of bliss. The raindrops around her freeze
in midair, the wolves stop baring their fangs.

For one second, the young girl marvels at her own invincibility.
But then it's fire, fire, always someone with a stake or a knife

ready to do her in. She is a spark about to go out.

Introduction to Hot Air Ballooning with Ruby Slippers

Part I: We're Not in Kansas Anymore

We have seen a lot of Technicolor lollipop nonsense
on our journey, me and the wizard.
It took tornadoes and hot air balloons to rip us from our humdrum.

Whatever you think of my sparkly shoes, their red gleam,
I had to kill to get them. A heavy price.
The wizard demanded the witch's head – and broom –

on a platter. I've become a bit bloodthirsty
along the yellow-brick pathway to Emerald City,
where now I reign, wizard by my side,

peddling his side-show remedies as spells these days
to a people helpless and twitching underneath the remote azure sky.
Anyone can ask Alice; retaining your sanity

in an alternate universe can really be a drain.
At least I've got my boys – lions, scarecrows, and tin men they may be,
but you know, they're loyal to the end, to death and beyond.

I'm having Glinda over for tea and advice:
how exactly can you remain remote and worshipped from a distance
for so many years without anyone asking questions?

I'm not looking for escape; my final wish was dominance.
My tee-totaling, dirt-farming aunt and uncle would barely recognize me now,
so far from Kansas and my gingham skirts. Toto growls majestic

from his satin pillow, and me, Oz's head witch, the bitch in charge,
no more pigtails and baskets, gumdrops and poppies
blooming and bowing in somnolent wonder.

Part II: Since Arriving in the Emerald City

I've found the constant rain to be a bit of a drag;
sure, it keeps the firs green and the poppies blooming,
but how many days of bright snowcapped mountains
and sunny shaggy-pony lollipop parades do we get each year?
Twelve, max? And two seasons: wet and less wet.
It seems the only way to reach me anymore is by hot air balloon,
and any day now I'm waiting for another lift-by-twister
to take me back to flatland, the gritty red dirt
of my Midwestern home, away from these azure seas
and rainbow-hued side streets. Toto's right at home;
more dogs than children in my magical town, the coffee's
sharp and hot, and no one remarks on my plaid pinafore and braids.
I'm an eco-warrior in ruby heels, with no Prince Charming
but four gay best friends who love to celebrate the solstice nude
riding down Fremont's yellow brick road on sparkly bicycles.
I'm thinking of taking up engine work at Boeing,
running circles around the wizard's palace in Medina,
maybe thinking up a new phone app: "Angry Flying Monkeys?"
Aunty Em, send me peaches and tomatoes grown in clay,
another round of Cheerwine and molasses cookies,
Uncle Henry's salty taciturn postcards from Branson stuck in the box.
I get tired of the brilliance, cherry blossom and rhododendron,
rainforests and recycling. Volvos and Suburus and bumper-sticker
left-wing politics and vegan cafes. Give me one more round
of farm-hand, of shooting range, of dry wheat field rustle and bluegrass
preachers on the AM before I relax into the Razzle-Dazzle of this new
Technicolor and techno-driven Metropolis, don my quirky glasses
and drink enough Oregon Pinot to wipe Kansas permanently off my map.

Part III: If I Stayed in Kansas, I Knew My Future

I'd end up married to a miner too young, or another farm hand
like my father, who died early in a tractor incident too gruesome
for anyone to describe to me – it was a lot worse
to imagine for a girl of fifteen with ribbons
still in her braids. My mother's factory fire
within months of my birth left me with memories
only of my aunts' unsmiling years canning, boiling,
scrubbing, milking cows and making biscuits.
So I ran after the man promising so much more,
mystical cures and balloon rides. You won't see me
again in Kansas, not middle-aged before my time,
rough-skinned, dirt in my throat and bitter on the tongue. No.
Let's say I went to Oz, an Emerald City.
Let's say I was blown by the wind.
Let's say it was all magical.

Introduction to Teen Girl Vampires

They turn feral while defending their human boyfriends, harmless and blond
in Varsity jackets and crew-cuts. These girls just want to be loved, and fed,

in that order, and can we blame them? A nurse here or there won't be missed,
or the guy playing "second policeman." Bram Stoker equated blood and sex,

Mina chaste and clever while hunting her Dracula down, his bite awaking
impulses that ignited and were ignored. These days, teen vampire girls enjoy sex

with abandon, tossing lovers around like tree limbs. These days, the girl
doesn't succumb to the monster, she is the monster, teeth gleaming in the moonligh

coquettish limbs and curls masking superpowers. Oh, she still wants to be
the prettiest girl at the prom, and perhaps she mourns some future idea

of motherhood. But men line up for the promise of her bite, her blood.
And she has nothing to fear; she cannot be broken, tarnished by age, her heart

impenetrable to anything except for that wooden stake.

Supervillain Studies: For the Love of Ivy

Poison Ivy Leaves a Note for Batman in the Wake of Another Apocalypse Attempt

You can see, can't you, the appeal of such a world – lush with growth,
an earth empty of men's trampling? In college, sitting through botanical medicine

classes, ecotoxicology, experiments in plant poisons – it became clear
that this was my verité – an orchid dressed to seduce wasps, a blooming

parasite wrapped around the trunk of a tree. You might take me home,
beg me for a kiss, but don't you see the xylem and phloem in my veins

can't pulse for you? My only offense not-death, regenerating from venom
fed me by my own professor? Feculent, fecund and feral, my power

you couldn't understand, being born of cave-dwellers, bats andhumans,
and your peculiar love of stray cats. My very existence my only crime

against nature. You can't stem the murmur of voices under soil,
buried against their will – radioactive trees, GMO fruit. Just consider me

another mutant gone wrong, my betrayals in the distant backstory, my tears
now flow a green ooze as I try to heal the land, cesium in the sunflowers,

goat genes welded into innocent corn. Despite drought and denial,
I will continue to grow unharmed, my defense all delicate leaf and toxic petal.

Introduction to the Body in Fairy Tales

The body is a place of violence. Wolf teeth, amputated hands.
Cover yourself with a cloak of leaves, a coat of a thousand furs,
a paper dress. The dark forest has a code. The witch sometimes
dispenses advice, sometimes eats you for dinner,
sometimes turns your brother to stone.

You will become a bird in a castle, but you'll learn plenty
of songs. Little girl, watch out for old women and young men.
If you don't stay in your tower you're bound for trouble.
This too is code. Your body is the tower you long to escape,

and all the rotted fruit your babies. The bones in the forest
your memories. The little birds bring you berries.
The pebbles on the trail glow ghostly white.

Zombie Stripper Clones:
They Are Not Regenerating

We are not zombies, thrown into a pool
of dubious origin and coming back beautiful
but decaying
unsure of how to live – pretending to swim,
eat yogurt like regular girls.

We are not clones, despite being drawn to specifications
(36-26-36) and bearing bouffants and bikinis
we might hack each other to pieces
but we are not confused about our identities

(living or not living) we continue
in this shape we were given
our cells cannot regenerate and the scientist
names us "Dead"
we are not regenerating
we cannot reproduce ourselves
we cannot be anything
but the fulfillment of your fantasy, flesh-eating or not.

Introduction to Conducting an Alien Autopsy

When you find the third heart beneath his carapace,
you start to wonder about the miracles of the system,
the circuits that keep our parts in place.

Once more, the trachea spasms, and he swallows;
once more, the gas bladder fills with air.
Is there anything more beautiful than this,

a foreign masterpiece, a secret hiding place
for all the universe? What will be revealed
by following this map into life on other planets?

For now, you listen to the whir and tick of his magnetic
insides, hear the engineers next door banging clumsily
on the outside of the metal spaceship, which refuses to divulge

its cargo. Dissection is an art, how taking things apart
is ultimately an exercise in putting things back together.

Hard Science

Introduction to Junk Science

Carl Sagan lied to you about the natural selection of crabs
with samurai faces, and Disney's cameramen threw those lemmings
over cliffs. Even the sub-atomic particles were a lie,
first three, now four, then dozens. Are quarks a mythology?
Pluto a non-planet, at most a moon? Remember:
once, top scientists believed the earth was flat,
leeches cured pneumonia, girls could not be color-
blind or dyslexic. Reserve your skepticism not just
for the annals of religion, or politics, but also for the article
about fish oil, that latest study on hematology. Remember:
policemen read skulls for evidence of murder.
Your experience may not be statistically significant.
Observation changes your outcomes. Measurement matters.

Introduction to Ecotoxicology, or, a Short History of the Chemical Age

Things fall apart; we cannot hear the tides
of perchlorates, heavy metals, phthalates
awash in lakes and drinking water.
From earthworm to architect, the mussel
and the monarch are excellent indicators.
Layers of bioaccumulation in prey
and predator, contaminants in flora and fauna.
The bees wander, dazed, from hives,
forgetting the path from flower to flower.
Desert birds lay eggs with shells too fragile
to contain their young safely, dead before they take flight.
Insect stings and mutated wheat – weals
on the skins of toddlers, angioedema
and immunotherapy. How much mustard sown
in the ground to leach cesium? Can we cure
a scientist with chelation? One more species adrift?

Can the blueberries be measured safe?
Explain to the woody cells of trees the presence
of pesticides in breast milk, the pale bodies
of fish turned upside down? Whisper of cancer
clusters, shadow of superfund sites, whole land
masses measured like a map of illness – here,
the caterpillars born without feelers, there, infants
with misshapen fingers. The sickness we inflict
on ourselves. What's one bluebird more or less,
one field of butterflies missed? Engineers chant
"risk assessment" as their test tubes chart
the limping birth of the rough end of a dark age.

On the 5th Anniversary of Fukushima, I'm Injected with Radioactive Blood Cells

And lie breathless beneath a gamma-ray camera.
They are tracing the lines of my red blood cells, photographing
the paths of the Technetium particles through my body...
brain, heart, thyroid, spleen, liver. Where did we go wrong?

I think of the radiation map of the ocean near Fukushima,
the pathways of contamination, Cesium-137 in the fish and sea lions,
the water that still pours, five years later, from the broken nuclear site,
an unhealed lesion, a seismic scar. Former beauticians
with Geiger counters test the dangers of home-grown carrots.

Einstein told us, "we...drift toward unparalleled catastrophes."
To radiate, to trace the rivers of destruction through our bodies,
our world. We trust the doctors, the governments;
we give our lives into their untrembling hands.

Welcome to the Sixth Extinction

It begins, not with rhinos or tigers in Southeast Asia,
but with plankton and coral in an acidified sea.
It begins with fungus killing chestnut trees,
then thousands of frogs.
It begins with a new Pangea, a flat earth, continents
connected not by land mass but by ship and jet,
a chain of human consequences, the uneaten fruit discarded,
the pets left feral on distant islands.
Will the fractured forests remain, or shrivel?
Will we, one dynamic but fragile species of our age,
become the last victim, comforting ourselves
with the hum of generators, air conditioners, radio waves?
The bones of dinosaurs lying in shallow desert graves
remind us: we were not here first, we will not be here last.

Introduction to Electromagnetics

We are attracted to one another by fundamental forces
not completely understood; I will try to rescue a boy
with mother issues; you will threaten your girlfriend's
abusive ex with a baseball bat in a dark alley.

Friction a power we underestimate; side by side,
we can't help but be at odds. Unlike charges attract,
like ones repel. So we cling to the rapscallion
at the school dance, or the Hitchcock blonde

married to the man next door. We have not learned
to interpret what's inside: the buzz, the chemical.
One atom shares its electron with another.
An impulse ripples through brain and muscle.

And so, a tower falls, a bomb explodes, we are all at war
with ourselves and each other. Surely there's a reason
for the bounce and chaos between our particle natures?
A current we cannot resist electrifies the air between us,

fuses at our fingertips, ready to ignite.

Introduction to Solar Weather, on Valentine's Day

At the peak of the sun's 11-year activity cycle,
solar flares will send a corona in the shape
of a heart hurtling towards earth on February 14,
a fiery embrace the planet cannot escape.
In the Netherlands, lovers will watch the aurora
with clasped hands, perhaps even unaware
of the sun's increased mania, that in another year
might disrupt satellites, electric grids, radio signals.
Watching a solar storm, we see only the warm glow
produced by the eruption of sun spots. We ignore
in our odd love affair with Northern lights,
the way poles might switch without warning,
those asteroids glancing off their trajectories,
the apocalyptic tone of spaceweather.com.

Women in the Sciences:
Hedy Lamarr Told to "Stop Silly Inventing"

Hedy, your image crackles even now on the screen
with your sharp accent, your incandescent brain.

How you tried so many years to train people to listen
to your ideas, hoping to break the code that would make men

see "spectrum communications" instead of your sparkle,
"frequency hopping" to help translate classified garble

into music. You told them you knew the dinner-party secrets of Stalin,
but they ignored your information, so you withdrew and stayed in -

playing piano with the boys, studying math and losing a few million.
Your famous figure, your face had to fade before your invention

was finally adopted by the Navy, after your patent had expired –
even that last victory denied. Communications permanently jammed.

Keeping your mouth shut was always hard, condemned
to temptress status, your glamour a screen,

your beauty a vault, your secret world hidden within.

Shorting Out

Like a radio   some of my connections have gone bad   fizzled
zapped and my legs won't move   in the direction I tell them
and sometimes when I mean to say "milk"   I say "snow"
    if I want "hairbrush"   I ask for "pomegranate"
It scares me   these white holes in my brain
where art or music might have been   maybe people's faces
    maybe whole sections of memory
I've studied circuits   electric impulse   the current flows and then it s t op s

creating gaps   shorting out

erasing memory   erasing impulse or   momentum or   motion detection

I put my foot down graceful as a dancer and the bones crack and collapse
my hands shake when I try to hold a pencil

at the edge of the electricity that is diminishing my neural network

can't preserve what I remember   the stumble   the forgetting

the wrong word in my mouth

when I try to say   your name

Introduction to Algebra

If X = your heart, and Y = the time away, what is the distance Z you still need to travel?

Your brother used to say about your father: "If he talks for more than five minutes, he starts speaking algebra."

If algebra is a foreign language, can you solve the country for Y?

In summer school a math teacher throws a desk at a student. If the desk weighs fifteen pounds, the teacher two hundred and ten, what is the internal pressure of a hot day trapped inside window panes and chalk lines?

Engineers and architects love it, you hear. And musicians. You think about music, about beat and count and the scrolling notes on the page. How many beats per minute of a butterfly's breath, how many arpeggios inside your lungs? You'd like to build a house and a bridge, you imagine the coefficients arcing into place elegantly, like a circular staircase.

You love geometry, the building of triangles, the circumscribing of paths. Water to air, hand to mouth. But the alphabet has abandoned you here. These symbols cannot lead you home.

Introduction to Time Travel Theory

Whether by string or tesseract, we humans interact with time
poorly – always a ghost instance waiting to disintegrate,
a missed opportunity for world peace or saving a parent

behind the scenes. Rips in the continuum, that's what we're built for,
to explore our "what if" Imaginariums, to wormhole our way
out of problems and ensure the miracle of our own birth,

the end of the war that destroys our planet. Who, what, where –when?
The planet tilts swiftly towards its own dark shadow self,
the universe in which there are no shrimp.

NASA invented and uninvented, Roswell's mysteries revealed
to be nothing but a future visit from earthlings to bestow
plastic and microwave technology. Flying saucers

nothing but a blurry reflection of our own hope
for an outside influence, for someone in some other future
to reveal the secrets that will spin us back on our proper axis, aliens

wise and benign enough to sleep in secret through their autopsies
while alternate-future-you rides a dragon into a time loop
or carries a samurai sword engraved with an important code

only you will be able to decipher.
Can you father the right child, kill the robot sent to doom
the future or program him for good, avoid crushing

that fragile butterfly beneath your inadvertent foot?
Who can promise us the unstable and tremulous path to truth,
justice, the American way, an apparatus that allows
a blissful and unknowing populace to, for once, survive?

A Primer for Your Personal Genome Project

A Primer for Reading 23 Pairs of Chromosomes, or, Introduction to Your Own Personal Genome Project

You are not a ticking time bomb.
Your results feel more like collage art,

a Frankenstein patchwork mostly unproblematic.
Yes, a carrier gene for this, a likelihood for that – an old age

of macular degeneration, a possible thyroid cancer –
but this book's chapters carry you in fascinating directions –

thousands of years into the past, exotic destinations and origins:
Ireland, Norway, France, even the Middle East and Africa.

Your skin color a trick of the light. Your statistics
are not so glum, and is it a delight or disappointment

to find you might have been born a blue-eyed blonde
instead of a grey-eyed brunette? To find a high pain tolerance

and no tendency towards alcoholism? Oh, speak to us,
amino-acid chains, and tell us our futures. Pretend for a moment

not to know our dark secrets, our fading memories
for foremothers. Embrace the order of things: traits

that take three neat pairings, a bleeding tendency ticked
on or off. A heart flutter your grandmother also experienced,

your great-aunt's straight nose and high forehead.
Sail into the future armed with the knowledge you refused

ignorance of your own body's demons and delights,
that your home country is fairy tale, ice and reindeer and green sheets

of rain, the sand of Brittany, the mountains of Tennessee.

Introduction to Field Studies

I am sorry. I am in the habit of leaving people without saying goodbye.
Leaving town in the middle of the school year.
Leaving before you know it.
Leaving without as much as a phone call.
I loved you and then I didn't and now I haven't ever said goodbye,
though it has been years. Because then you were optimistic,
and I had already shut the door. Goodbye to all that.
Don't look back. Don't look behind you. Too often
there are monsters on the threshold. If you don't look back
you can't be caught. And anyway, the future is an endless horizon.

Even if it wasn't that great; it all looked promising, once.
New jobs, new clothes, new lawns to mow,
new fields to study and specimens to capture.
New neighborhood bars to try – one Greek
with wonderful tomato salad, another Cuban
where they made caprihainas. I don't do nostalgia, my darling.
When I look back, it is only in dreams, where you remain a thin,
dusky-eyed teenager, smirking at my performances.
I still remember your favorite lines from books,
underlined in blue pen: *I dreamed my lady came and found me dead.*
I am sorry. I cannot look back. Monsters in the closet.
I don't even remember your last name. I am older.
My life is not what it should have been.
I've thrown out all my suits and work on not remembering the words.
Sometimes the yard is so sweet with jasmine it overwhelms me.
I've gone all the way to the edge, you see, where they grow
oranges and avocadoes and the sun always shines.
Next door they grow grapes. I joke I am a wine grape,
with their need for gentle weather. There is nowhere left to go
now except back. And I won't be looking back.

Introduction to California Poetics

In a place of perpetual climate control
you cannot get too angry at the world
you cannot get too angry at ranunculus
who throw their wide unfragrant faces to the light
you cannot be angry with the hummingbirds
who winter here, confusing feeders with fuschias,
or the girls who wear hot pants with shearling boots
in January. You cannot be angry, even with
the water crisis, with all the swimming pools
and sprinklers, with the careless swerving
of giant cars from lane to lane. You will eat
your avocado or asparagus, your citrus straight
from the tree, you will see the goats and grapevines,
you cannot be angry, with all this blue sky, dimmed
hardly at all by the brown layer of smog,
with the hard sunlight glinting off the cold ocean,
the unwelcoming skin of the date palm,
the oleander continuing to bloom along highways.
You will not wear a sweater and huddle by a notebook.
You will ski, or swim, you will hike by giant eucalyptus trees,
you will startle egrets and pelicans in a salt marsh,
you will forget you ever wrote books at all,
you will no longer regret, you will throw away your sweaters
and burn down your library, you will go mad
tearing at the easy beauty, the soft golden sheen of skin,
you will break the earth itself, turning to dust, unremembered.

Introduction in Indigo Children
(After a Consult with a Medical Intuitive)

—for K.R. Agodon

You kept making posters of women with
rose petals across their eyelids, then went blind.
I consulted a medical psychic who told me
I was an indigo child, great with promise, that
a star entered my body at birth. A blue-cloaked
Virgin Mary whirls above me in the air
like a dancing queen. Like Nelson Mandela and
Joan of Arc, I should expect both great work and great suffering.
Indigo children, like Ragdoll kittens, may or may not be
part-alien, with independent natures and high IQs.
We usher in the Age of Aquarius, and here all I can picture
is the musical "Hair," you with daisies over your eyes
and around your blond locks a halo and me glowing blue
in the dark, letting the sunshine in. Never mind my little brother
is the actual Aquarian, typically diffident, not at all
the whirling dervish. We decide spinning Marys are better
than angels with flaming swords, an icon of music and celebration,
and hope I can, unlike Mandela and poor Jeanne, avoid prison.
We pray for epiphany, a star to light the way and stumble,
unmindful, on a path twisted, littered with mystic trouble.

Introduction to Sex and Death

On our honeymoon we became adventurers,
riding horses across steep dry trails where they lost
their footing, navigating whitewater in frail rafts.
I caught your foot as you were nearly jostled overboard
(you couldn't swim) and we come out wet and cold,
muscles so sore hours in a hot cedar tub could not cure us.
At 5 AM we rode a balloon over mountains,
assumed crash positions as it landed uneasily
over sharp rocks. I took you fishing and got a wedge
of old splintered fence in my arm, we went to the hospital
to get it cut out with a scalpel. My first tetanus shot
in ages. Looking back I understand our youthful desperation
to stay armed and dangerous, to rappel down cliffs
and sail over rooftops, to catch butterflies at high altitudes,
our desire to stay superhuman a little longer,
before we settled into jobs and lives
that seemed too permanent, too safe, too mortal
for our still glittering twenty-something bodies.

Yearbook: Not Pictured

Not pictured: the way your breath felt. The heat of your stomach against mine. That terrible strawberry-scented smoke at the school dance that never fully masked that sweaty-gym smell. The way your face was always obscured.

Not pictured: the hours we spent learning HyperCard and Pascale, languages obsolete before they were assimilated. Hulking beasts, those old computers, wrangling cords around wrists and ankles.

Not pictured: The reason my brother is looking away from the camera. The feelings you actually had for that girl with her long legs next to yours, arms casually slung around shoulders.

Not pictured: That we never said goodbye. No signatures in the yearbooks, nothing and after all these years I still want to say *stop, stop.*

Not pictured: Bar Mitvahs where you learned to listen to Hebrew scripture, ate smoked salmon and danced around chocolate fountains. Pizza parties, roller skating parties, parties where you helped the parents make beer cheese dip, parties where everyone got in the hot tub with leaves floating in it in their underwear at midnight and you thought in the right lighting everyone's bodies look beautiful.

Not pictured: The way your hands shook before French class. The hours we spent together huddled over the single library copy of *Rolling Stone* when we were supposed to be learning our lines. How clear your eyes were, almost teal, like an alien.

Not pictured: the way the senior girls protected me from those girls who threatened to beat me up after that basketball game. How I learned to take off my bra underneath my shirt on the bus. The most important lessons are not the ones we were graded for; you were better in math than you thought you were and worse at languages.

Not pictured: Sneaking out to lie in the sun under the pink dogwood tree, an aberration in the clean landscaping of the ugly squat school with its jagged shade and the way the flowers' irregular edges cut the blue sky.

Not pictured: The girl who threw your class ring into a lake. She got pregnant and didn't finish school. The boy that died in that car accident – the last time he smiled at you, it was like saying goodbye. The friend who died from cancer last year. You never make it to any reunions.

From the archives: You keep these pages for some reason. In case someone needs to look up what we were really like back then, an archive of terrible haircuts and fashions. Allusions to the pastimes of American youth including: drugs, field hockey, literary magazines, cutting class, deliberate dilettantism and debauchery, sprained ankles on the field, the realization that your bones have always been that way, that you aren't a recent creation. Really, you've been there all along.

As Venus and Jupiter Come Together, We Fall Apart

It used to be we would star-watch together, but lately I find myself
searching the night sky alone. Looking for a sign? Looking for a way out.

The solar storms bring the Northern Lights to our horizon,
but you don't see them. They glow blue and orange, colors not even

visible on your spectrum. Spectral, magnetic storms cause disruptions,
draw our hearts more distant. I bang my head against the landscape;

suburban sprawl out every window, fires burning on the television.
How many churches destroyed? How many of us spinning apart?

I used to want to die. I would wait for life to trickle out of me, a little
at a time. Lately I've been watching the moon, reflecting back my own face,

pale, waxing and waning, always alone. She doesn't know or care about us.
The two planets appear shining, so close they are almost one star now,

but this is an illusion. They are in distant orbit, isolated in their dusty,
unbreathable atmospheres, unable to stand, ever, to touch.

Introduction to Dream Interpretation

Dreams about hurricanes and bears are a warning. Don't take any unnecessary risks. Your emotions are powerful and destructive.

Never write about dreams. There is nothing more boring than other people's dreams.

Last night Rita Dove was teaching me about music in a dream. She asked about my mother, showed me how to draw concentric circles that celebrated order in the universe.

If you dream that a seal visits you on land, this means you have two natures. It is a sign of transformation. One of you might love the water, which represents the subconscious.

I was talking to you in a dream, you were telling me not to worry. I haven't seen you in twenty years, but you were somehow older than seventeen, you had grown up away from me.

Is your dream a metaphor, or perhaps a symbol? Or a visual pun? Jung believed he communed with God in his sleep. Freud believed everything was about his mother. Beware foxes flying out your window; fractals indicate creativity.

I've dreamed for years about being interrupted in the middle of a shower. Showering in a dream might represent healing, or a spiritual cleansing. What does it mean if I always end the dream annoyed because there's still shampoo in my hair?

Try lucid dreaming. Keep a dream dictionary by the bed. Try to switch on the lights to see if you are still dreaming; electricity never works in dreams. You may accidentally find the path to your future in the two sentences you write while half-asleep.

Find yourself a good oracle. If seven skinny cows eat seven fat cows, you might want to watch out for the king's wife. Angels or demons might be involved. If the angel is spinning, it's time to pay attention.

End Times Eschatology

A Narcissist's Apocalypse

If my own light is burning out, then it feels right
that the earth should too. Shut down the sun,
let the crops wilt and suffer. As my blood stops running,
so too should the rivers and seas, no longer reliable
in their courses, no longer teeming with life. My spirit
is dim as this forever-twilight and the animal inside me
noses around the forest, confused. If this is the end,
let me tell the story. Let me write it in stone, send it out
into the universe on a rocket. Rage, rage against the dying.
Go supernova. Once I twirled my hair in my fingers,
once my lips kissed other lips dry and warm. Once my heart
beat and the world spun on its axis. Nothing wobbled.
Nothing was uncertain. There was a house on a street
with a smiling sky above. There were wars and rumors of wars.
Mass extinctions. Yes, the occasional earthquake, tsunami, tornado.
Yes, the occasional storm, the crying out, asking for attention.
But now, everything quivers, restless and itching, waiting
for the final signal, the shutdown, the last penetrating burst,
the eyelids stuttering closed, the last breath exhaled, the soul unlit.

The Last Love Poem

I am obsolete as my ancestors, the Appalachian glass blowers,
provoking fire over and over to produce their artifacts.

I knew no writing could survive when we started calling children "vectors,"
when our own forests grew heavy with toxic spores.

A map? A list? A series of images? What could I write now
that would do anything? A poem orphaned, a crystalline ornament

with no Christmas in sight, swirled with delicate color, resting
gently on a ledge until the inevitable smash…

So here in my last moments, let me set down my memories of you:
your rough skin, your green eyes, your slightly clumsy hands.

We turned and smiled at each other on the ugly concrete glinting with broken glass
as someone yelled obscenities and someone else handed out pizza slices to strangers.

When we ran out of flour, we learned to bake cookies out of nuts, seeds, flowers.
We decided, against all odds, to plant dahlias.

Do you see this as a rebellion? That after all this, the poet clings, stubborn,
to romance, to the idea that somehow a small connection,

a tiny universe of fire and friction, might be preserved?

Post-Apocalypse Postcard (with HGTV Magazine)

The houses line up in neat rows, uniform and crisp. We wonder how to dress, like Scarlett O'Hara, cutting up the drapes in the demolition. The color schemes run towards camouflage. The fires destroyed so much except the beachfronts and mountain treehouses, the millionaires' mansions mangled behind vast gates. Everyone fled the cities; now we look for country charm, for provisions, for a secret bunker of canned food and Cipro. Try the islands of Washington State, where the whales still call mournfully, or the snow-caps of Whistler, with tidy condos next to fresh spring water and equipped with generators. If you must roam the streets of Detroit, Chicago, Cincinnati, be warned the dogs have all gone feral and have eaten all the white-tailed deer. Sometimes a patch of community garden remains intact, like a beacon, but mostly it's barbed wire and looted, boarded storefronts. Which of us was trained to go off the grid, in a land free of cell phones or running water? Camping by lakes in the thousands, refugees bargain hunt among empty houses, a lamp or a map or a mouthful of mashed potatoes. We wonder through our neighbors' carefully showcased homes, fixed up to sell, vacant-eyed: wondering – gas or wood-burning? Was the safe still sealed? There's a lone shoe on a staircase, the last vestige of someone's question: take or leave? What, in the end, is essential baggage?

An Introduction to Salvation

Are you ready to be saved? It's best to do it
here, by the water, where the pure white spirit descends upon you
like a dove. Or out in the desert, among the stars and locusts.
In the trenches, too, that's a popular choice.

Are you truly ready, my brother, my sister?
What is the cost now that we are in our darkest hour,
here at the end of civilization and all that we can hear
is the sad broken slap of water wheel upon water,

the sound of malfunctioning machinery?
We dream of robots, of zombies, of plagues and comets,
of tidal waves that wipe out our world. We dream of the end
because we long to disappear. We keep building bombs,

lighting fires, pulling dead children from dead women in muddy fields.
Do you claim your hands are clean? But look at the blood
you've spilled just to get here. You'll never be quite free
no matter how you pray. You'll never claw the scales from your eyes.

Job Interview at EndTimes ExpressSystemics (A Subsidiary of the RadiantZMax Corporation)

Thriving self-starters wanted! Desired skill set:
building fires, setting traps, fashioning weapons
out of unused office furniture. Prepare for the death-match
lightning round against your competition,
the mild-looking man in a navy blue suit. Don't miss
the puppy pen and trampoline room for those
who can avoid the burning lava. Join a winning team!
We're looking for bright-eyed innovators who can talk
their way out of the war room. Please remember the water cooler
is for executives only; all others must drink their own urine.
Prepare a demonstration of your passion for technology
by building your own battlebot. Look to our company
to lead you into the future—leather visors and t-shirts for all!
Located off 1-75 between Hill of Blazing Skulls and Chuck-E-Cheez.

Notes From Before the Apocalypse

There was a halo around a Gibbous moon.

The horses all lay down in their fields.

Children died in a school holding hands.

Tornadoes right through the city centers ripped up everything
we had built.

The hives of bees were empty. (Do Not Fly Apart)

The bridges collapsed, leaving people stranded.

There were knife attacks, guns in malls and theaters, bombings at the races. Flus,
pneumonias, resistant bacteria, virulent strains.

Every day in spring the snakes flew through the grass.

We could not escape.

And all we dreamed of was death. A plague. A Warning sign. Sporadic shaking.
Moons out of orbit. Water in the basements. Earthquakes along state lines. Our
bones grew cold while we slept. There was no distraction. Everyone threatening
a different weapon. Nature turned on us, furious. We had a bad case of burnout.
Then no sleep at all.

We tried to hold together. We prayed. We lit candles. We huddled for warmth.
We marshaled resources. We held hands. We looked to the animals. Someone
told me to pull it together. I was busy writing down the stories. Even with the
barns burning, the last glow on the horizon, I could not stop taking notes.

Post-Apocalypse Christmas Card

It's hard to picture snow here on the sand, nothing but a frosting of ice on the seagrass. The wind and water bite with cold this time of year. I threw a bunch of cranberries in boiling water, just to see what they would do, the pop and color. I miss seasons and pine trees, mittens and sleigh bells, the piped-in caroling, even if they were all artificial. The shiny paper and useless baubles, the lights during the long evenings together. I know you won't remember when we decorated a branch with red pepper lights and ate spaghetti for Christmas Eve, but that's the memory that stays with me now, too-sweet marinara and sitting on bare floors. I wrap myself in your old plaid flannel shirt with a basket of the last oranges, and watch the water, stretching in early sunset blue and empty.

But It Was an Accident

Yes, I was the one who left out the open petri dishes of polio and plague next to the pasta.

I leaked the nuclear codes, the ones on the giant floppy disks from 1982.

I fell asleep at the button. I ordered tacos and turned out the lights. How was I to know that someone was waiting for the right time?

I thought the radio was saying "Alien attack" and headed for the fallout shelter, and failed to feed the dogs.

I followed evacuation plans. I just followed orders. I was the pilot of the bomber, I was the submarine captain, I steered into the iceberg. I held the scalpel but I was shaking. I was the one in charge. I was on the red phone saying "Do it" decisively.

I always imagined writing propaganda; how could I possibly see what was coming when they dropped the fliers, when the angry mobs began choking people in the street? I was always good at creating a panic.

I never saw the Ferris wheel start its fatal roll. I looked away just as the plane plummeted, as the building burned. I shook my head at disaster, afraid to meet.

It was just an accident. It was fate. It was never my hand on the wheel. When you point fingers, point them towards the empty sky.

Post-Apocalypse Postcard with Love Note

I still look at the locket you gave me when I wake,
wearing its metal down with my touch. I can't
communicate with the mutants but just knowing
they're out there is a comfort. You know, a continuum.
I remember the last night on the beach, our lips, the sand
beneath our fingertips, the cries of monkeys in the jungle.
We thought we had outrun it but the earth crumbled
just as we were finding the light. I'm toasting you again
with the last of the champagne. I feel a little less alive
each morning. Every stone becomes a church.
Every star that winks out is named after you.

Remnant

I knew I was home when I walked down a path
of decaying leaves, through a bridge of tree limbs.
You couldn't even drive on this path that led me home.
That made sense as I'd always liked the country,
the far-awayness and difficulty of it, the chance
of your neighbor pulling a gun on you or on another neighbor,
the chance that the smoke in the air was someone burning leaves
or maybe burning their house down for the insurance.
Yes, that's my idea of home – picking around the remains
of someone's burned-down house for the chance of finding
really good wild strawberries there, little patches of violets,
the trinkets of divestment. You never get lonely in the woods.
I've never been frightened of bears, they left me alone,
or the birds. There's the comfort of the knocking on hollow
branches, the scratching song of insects, and those tubes
of sunlight that show up on the path, lighting the way.

Post-Apocalypse Postcard from Appalachian Chalet

I've got my head next to a granite-strewn stream that gurgles amid sunbeams as if the whole world never went wrong. As if nothing. I've got at least two crates of Coca-Cola stashed inside, a pile of Little Debbie Swiss Cake Rolls, all the beef jerky I can eat. A few bears have come by, mostly uninterested, tearing through the old garbage. There are leaves and mist and no noise except the wind and once in a while, an eerie whine – foxes? ghosts? If I smell the air I can believe. This is where I came in childhood to hide away. I loved the fossil rocks jutting at all angles, the tangled mountainsides full of deciduous trees. The butterflies are gone, of course, but the cicadas still hum inside their shells, oblivious. If only you were here with me. I'm far past the florescent dinosaur mini-golf and pancake restaurants, quiet now, too far from ski slopes and tourist traps to matter. Without traffic, the paved roads all seemed too lonely. If it all dies down, I thought, this is where I'd want my bones, here where the shadow of the mountains falls, in a valley of daffodils, in a chamber of forest so vast the only things to meet me will be wild things.

The End of the Future

Looks bleaker than we thought. The end is near, all those signs.
The clouds outside my house curl like an evil magician's beard.

The children's books are full of futuristic dystopias. Clones, slaves,
hunger games, post-nuclear mutants, zombies. It's not a safe era,

they've been taught to fear everything – salmonella in the peanut butter,
allergens in the air, the creepy guy next door who, let's face it, probably

is a pervert. They know better than to say "yes" to adults.
So let's leave it to them to survive whatever rapture or apocalypse

lies before them. Let us accumulate for them: potato chips, underwear,
stories that were written before paper, eyeglasses and antibiotics.

A narrative of how things used to be. An imagined world without wars
or time paradoxes or plagues, where they could camp out all night and watch fireflies

before the green glow came to represent something far more sinister.

At the End of Time (Wish You Were Here)

I tried to call you one night but you were in Thailand.
I was listening to Tool's "Opiate" and reading about the particulate
levels in China and the meteor that had narrowly missed us yesterday
and realized I'd missed the recent eclipse and also missed you.

I realized 40 years of learning were leaking through the lesions in my brain,
names and faces and memories of us and I wanted to reassure you
that I would still remember you but then maybe I won't. Like the radioactive
water leaking from Fukushima, burning the algae and sea lions –

nature takes what it wants from us. And what have we learned
that will do us any good, standing here on the brink of fire and flame,
of disaster, of zombie movie dystopia and plague and final girls:
what will we hold onto? At the end all we have is ourselves

and sometimes not even that. We must be our own saviors.
We must wield the axe against the assassin that is death and time,
that is endings and goodbyes, chop down the difficulties
and the disappointments until the wall is gone, until we are back

in the sunlit yards of our childhoods, when we could still cry
without irony and sweet things still tasted sweet and my limbs
didn't end in numbness, remember that? If we can still remember,
then somewhere things must be better than here. Wish you were here.

Post-Apocalypse Postcard from an Unnamed Island in the Pacific Northwest (in the style of Basho)

After Appalachian escapes and L.A. adventures, I've landed here, at the northern damp edge of our continent. The evergreens cling to bare dirt, rock, and scrub, a lesson in survival. I've run out of meds, of food, of energy to keep running. I'm in a cabin on the edge of the water. The hawks here have persisted, rabbits plentiful here where so little has changed.

I think I saw a deer -
bare patches on its fur and scrawny,
but still. It rains and rains.

The sea and sky and branches wet and murky. I was watching storms through the glass walls of this abandoned home, all slate shower and granite kitchen, generator and solar coils. There is still heat coming through the floors, from a safer time. I huddle under a stack of old blankets, some of them with children's patterns that make me think "whose?" and then…There's a well that contains clean water, there are reminders of uncontaminated earth:

a flash of movement
in the blackberry thicket -
a black fox face.

To the Ends of the Earth

Here I am standing on the end as far as a year of traveling
by foot, by rowboat, by car after car abandoned
on the side of the road would take me.
I've been sending you postcards in mailboxes
that will never be emptied knowing you will never read them
never see them never see me again.
I'm looking out into blankness the black water the sky
quiet silent oppressive…I am leaning over the edge
like these trees trunks blackened by fire or blight their roots
barely gripping the land any more.
Would you follow me to the ends of the earth?
I've found hollows, libraries to sleep in, slipped
into abandoned museums to escape the cold,
lay my face on marble floors. Walked through shoes
and worn out blankets, eaten from supply closets,
lit candles in cabins, found solar flashlights in the dark.
I've learned maps of matches and bottled water, iodine and Cipro.
I've packed so much in to these final days and you never found me.
You may not even be here anymore, just one more
of my memories retreating, fond and warm, like Christmas,
like movie theatre popcorn, like the spinning lights
above a dance floor full of bodies flailing in celebration, in preparation.

Grieving

This is how I grieve: I take pictures of trees.
I may be saying goodbye with photographs.
Here, a branch of pink blooms against a blue sky,
and a petal against the lens. There, the whirl
of violent camellia against the dark green leaves.
I want to remember what it is about earth
that I might miss. You, standing tall underneath
the branches, among the flowers, smiling.
I taste each bite of fruit sadly, the bite of sour plum
or the mild sweetness of melon, like I might forget.
I can't write you a note about this, I won't say
So long, farewell, like I'm going on a trip.
All I can do is capture these reminders, frame by frame,
these calls to life, to bleeding and feeding and ferociously
taking up space and time. *Here,* these flowers say, *here we were.*

Epilogue: A Story for After

I want to tell you a story about how we survived the end of the world. Crouched around a dying fire, I illustrate with shadow puppets the old, beat-up van, the velocity of water and sky, the unnamable odds against us. What really sells it? The way the ending goes on forever, moon ebbing closer to the mysterious dark, its craggy face calling out, the skies scattered with falling stars. The way objects are nearer than they appear. You next to me, and I remind you – here is where we used to be, here is where we are. I draw a line in the dirt with a fork and draw a picture – a house made of a square and a triangle, a single daisy in the yard, and two smiling stick figures. This is what we dreamed of, the day we awaited has arrived. There are no more shotguns or dusty trails lined with diseased corpses. A ship arrives on top of a mountain, heralded by doves; an airplane lands on another planet, seatmates dazed by the lack of gravity. We might teach the dragons to dance, learn the alchemy of soil again, rebuild libraries with tales of fantastic voyage. All I need right now is you, the simple weight of your hand, the warmth of your breath, and this last cup of coffee to tell me – we are miraculous.

Also by Jeannine Hall Gailey

Becoming the Villainess

She Returns to the Floating World

Unexplained Fevers

The Robot Scientist's Daughter

The Moon City Poetry Award

2014 Sad Math
by Sarah Freligh

2015 Field Guide to the End of the World
by Jeannine Hall Gailey

Printed in the USA
CPSIA information can be obtained
at www.ICGtesting.com
JSHW020104081023
49545JS00004B/201

9 780913 785768